AMBASSADOR
# JAMES (WALLY) BREWSTER


# ELEVATING TOUGH CONVERSATIONS

## A Field Guide for Effective Communications

Editorial direction by Anne Bruce

Edited by Phyllis Jask

Cover design by Flip Design Studio

Interior graphic design by Brenda Hawkes

Author photo by Fernando Calzada

Printed in the United States of America

ISBN-13: 978-1-7330779-2-7

# Introduction

The world is a wonderful and dynamic place. It is full of unimaginable opportunities, but one key step to achieving those is to push through our fears and elevate tough conversations to transform our lives.

From the second we were born and our eyes connected with others in the room, we began our life's communication. As we grew up, a series of life events and DNA influenced our level of communication and how we engaged with others in all aspects of our personal and professional relationships.

How we communicate defines a significant part of our personal brand.

Ambassador James (Wally) Brewster

I'm no stranger to elevating a tough conversation. As a diplomat and business executive, I am required to elevate tough conversations in all aspects of my communication. I will share with you a small piece of my journey that forced me to face many tough conversations.

After spending years building a career in the private sector, I was appointed as U.S. Ambassador to the Dominican Republic from 2013 until January 20, 2017. I had many tough conversations during my tenure, as ambassadors often do. My story is unique because I'm the only openly gay Ambassador to be appointed in the Western Hemisphere to date, and as such, my presence in this conservative country was not viewed as a positive thing by many in power, especially influential religious leaders like the Cardinal and his Bishops. They relentlessly worked to discredit me and the work I was doing as a representative of the United States. The tough conversations I had regarding corruption, equality, human rights, and homophobia were welcomed on the world stage, but not so much by my adversaries in-country.

When addressing these and many other issues, I followed the four pillars that I outline in this book. They are simple yet effective strategies you can use to elevate tough conversations in your life, too.

You hold in your hand a guide to elevating the tough conversations you may face in your life—be they interpersonal confrontations, family dynamics, office politics, everyday rudeness, or even discrimination.

Using these pillars will allow you to show people who you really are, what you value, what your purpose is, and most importantly, that you can and will use your voice. When you practice using these pillars, you will elevate your brand and continue to change your world and the world we live in through the great value you bring to every situation you approach in life.

My journey is unique, and so is yours. If you use these simple pillars I developed, I am confident you will see great success.

# What is elevating a tough conversation anyway?

I believe elevating the conversation is as important now as it ever was. Promoting inclusiveness, diversity, respect, and dignity is inspiring and is needed around the world. Too often today we see conversations that are contentious and argumentative often resulting at an impasse. The remedy, of course, is to elevate the conversation, reach a consensus, and move your initiative forward.

**Elevating a tough conversation means using your voice to stand up for what you believe in.**

It's taking a risk and speaking up for yourself or someone else.

It's standing up for what's right. It's being brave. It's engaging your brain and your heart in the conversation.

And it's using diplomacy—the art of communicating with people in an insightful, effective, and empathetic way. You see, diplomacy isn't just for those of us in the political arena!

Before we discuss the steps to elevating tough conversations, answer the following questions about some of your most recent experiences. It will help you as we go through the steps to follow.

4

When did you last find yourself having a tough conversation?

How did you handle it?

_______________________________________________

_______________________________________________

_______________________________________________

_______________________________________________

What was the outcome?

_______________________________________________

_______________________________________________

_______________________________________________

_______________________________________________

What tough conversations do you anticipate having in the future?

___________________________________________

___________________________________________

___________________________________________

___________________________________________

What concerns you most about having this conversation?

___________________________________________

___________________________________________

___________________________________________

___________________________________________

## What outcome would you like to see from this conversation?

# Four Pillars of Elevating a Tough Conversation

**1.** Be self-aware and speak your truth.

**2.** Do not hide in a crowd.

**3.** Bring in your allies to have your back.

**4.** Achieve the unachievable!

Pillar One

Be Self-Aware
and Speak Your
Truth

This pillar combines two interconnected concepts: self-awareness and speaking your truth. It boils down to this: you can only speak your truth if you're self-aware. **Self-awareness is the key to building long-lasting relationships, finding a career that suits you, and growing yourself to your highest potential.** This is the foundational pillar that will help you elevate tough conversations.

Self-awareness in my life has been critical, but never more critical than when the Cardinal and his Bishop in the Dominican Republic appeared on national television and called me a "faggot" and said, "His kind are not welcome here and if he comes he will suffer and be forced to leave."

I had to be self-aware that every move I made would define not just me but also those who were marginalized, my Christianity, and the strength of the United States. With my husband, we quickly determined we would be visible and speak to our faith, our pride in our marriage, and our pride as representatives of our great nation. You see, my God is one of love and I am proud of who I am and I would neither apologize nor be threatened. At that point, speaking and standing in my truth was critical for many reasons.

12

When have you had to speak your truth?

______________________________________________

______________________________________________

______________________________________________

______________________________________________

How critical was self-awareness to the
conversation?

______________________________________________

______________________________________________

______________________________________________

______________________________________________

Why do you believe having self-awareness can help you elevate a tough conversation?

______________________________

______________________________

______________________________

______________________________

______________________________

______________________________

# Self-Awareness

Part one of this pillar is to have tough conversations with yourself first. I encourage you to be authentic and absolutely and completely true to yourself at all times.

Are you satisfied with things as is, or do you want more...not only for yourself, but for your friends, colleagues, community, or nation? Are you achieving your goals, or better yet—achieving the unachievable? Are you doing what you want in life? Are you fulfilled by what you do?

Think about this: If you can't speak your truth to yourself, are you going to be perceived as credible to anyone else? Are you honest with yourself? Why or why not?

_______________________________________________

_______________________________________________

_______________________________________________

_______________________________________________

_______________________________________________

_______________________________________________

Is fear holding you back from realizing your true potential? (Put a pin in this...I'll talk a little more about fear in a bit.)

Please take a moment to reflect on these questions as well as the ones that follow, and write your answers below. When you do you will be heightening your self-awareness quotient.

__________________________________________

__________________________________________

__________________________________________

__________________________________________

__________________________________________

__________________________________________

It's difficult to tell others about who you really are, what you value, and what your purpose is if you don't know what you stand for.

Think about your life for a moment. What do you stand for? What do you hold true? What do you value most?

________________________________

________________________________

________________________________

________________________________

________________________________

________________________________

Here's a point of caution: Will others listen to you if they suspect you're not being genuine? If you're not self-aware, you may be perceived as false or unauthentic, or worse, labeled a hypocrite. As such, you may likely lose any power to influence others and lose the ability to have your voice heard.

**Be authentic and know yourself first.**

Seek your own answers and verify your facts— don't rely on the opinion of others to form your beliefs. Many of us do that, and that's really just silencing your own voice.

Think for yourself because you should practice self-accountability. You still have to look at yourself in the mirror. Do you like who you see? Are you on the right path for you? How do you make your peace with yourself?

________________________________

________________________________

________________________________

________________________________

________________________________

________________________________

# It takes self-awareness to speak your truth.

Remember, self-awareness has to come from within you. Take the necessary time to get to know yourself, be honest with yourself, and acknowledge the things that you hold most dear.

# Speak Your Truth

Part two of this pillar is you must speak your truth. I will bet you know right from wrong. It should not take a huge, internal moral dilemma for you to make a conscious choice to execute the right thing. That's where the element of self-awareness comes into play.

If you are confident in your beliefs and you know who you are, you are less likely to doubt yourself, and therefore, more able to speak your truth and more able to handle any resulting conflict or friction. Speaking your truth also shows you can be genuine, the real deal, transparent and truthful.

Speak your truth in a diplomatic way so people will receive your message and intent. Disagreements happen. They are part of life. Elevating a conversation does not have to be awkward, contentious, or confrontational. Name-calling, ranting, or trolling are no ways to get your point across. You do not have to villainize people whose opinions differ from yours. There's more than a sprinkle of truth to the old adage "you catch more flies with honey than with vinegar." That does not mean you have to be nice to those who are mean or have opinions or portray actions that are offensive. It just means if you speak to your truth, their ugliness will shine even brighter. As former First Lady Michelle Obama stated, "When they go low, we go high." That statement is one everyone should live by.

# Facing Fears

The prospect of speaking your truth out loud can sometimes make you quake with fear. Stick with me here as I talk about fear, because it's the number one thing that's going to silence your voice if you let it.

Speaking your truth leaves you vulnerable and exposed. Fear puts you on lockdown, stifling your voice and rendering you speechless.

I'll let you in on a secret: **Your voice has value. Your voice should be heard.**

24

Describe a time when you had to speak your truth toward positive change. What did you say that was effective? What could you have improved? How did fear affect what you said or didn't say?

___________________________________________

___________________________________________

___________________________________________

___________________________________________

___________________________________________

___________________________________________

Weigh your fears against this critical question:

**What are you so afraid of that not speaking your truth is the better choice?**

Fear is behind so many of the things you do and even don't do. Let's look at three big fears that might be hanging you up.

- **Fear of the unknown:** What's going to happen to you if you open your mouth? How will others react to what you just said? What's going to happen to you, your loved ones, your community, your country?

■ **Fear of consequences:** Some are big, others small, but all are real. What's the immediate fallout going to look like? Will you lose your family, friends, or job? Will you be harmed physically, mentally, or financially?

■ **Fear of looking foolish:** Sometimes subconsciously we fear embarrassment. And that's a natural thing that can occur in tough conversations. Do you hold your tongue for fear of looking foolish?

How do you face your fears so you can  speak your truth and elevate a tough conversation? Nobody knows what could happen, and like physics, to every action there's an equal and opposite reaction.

It's been said that acknowledging a problem is the first step in overcoming it. This applies to fear, too.

The way I see it, you have three choices when facing fear (or making any decision, really): the right choice, the wrong choice, or no choice at all.

The risky part is figuring out which choice is the right one for you or your situation. You can choose to acknowledge—but not act on—or ignore your fear and move on. Sometimes you'll choose right, other times wrong.

**But making no choice at all, or choosing the status quo, is actually making a choice as well. Fear hangs you up when you choose "no choice at all" because you're declining to take a risk for fear of making the wrong choice.**

# But you'll never know until you try.

Speaking your truth doesn't come naturally to a lot of people. It may be uncomfortable for you. But that doesn't make it any less necessary in life. You must get comfortable with the uncomfortable. Because if you don't tackle the tough conversations, who will? If you don't ask the hard questions, who will? If you opt out, who's going to make a change? **The question is: If not me, if not you, then who?**

I have a bit of advice:

- Be brave.

- Be vulnerable.

- Be resilient.

Take a risk and try not to let your fear grip you into paralysis and inaction. Making a choice to speak your truth despite any fear you may be feeling is better than doing nothing at all. And even if you make the wrong choice for your situation, you still win because you took the risk to try a different approach.

Describe a time you took a risk that paid off during a tough conversation.

____________________________________________

____________________________________________

____________________________________________

____________________________________________

____________________________________________

32

Sometimes fear wins. If you could turn back the clock to a situation where you didn't say anything but wish you had, what would you have said? If you had a do-over today, would you speak up? Why or why not?

________________________________________

________________________________________

________________________________________

________________________________________

________________________________________

________________________________________

**Being self-aware will help guide your decision-making when it comes to facing down any fears you might have when you encounter something or someone different, unfamiliar, or disagreeable.** If you are committed to elevating tough conversations, you can act despite your fears. That's being brave.

I know how difficult it is to be brave or diplomatic when your knee-jerk reaction is to turn away in the spirit of self-preservation. But being brave doesn't mean you're not afraid; it means you're afraid and you do what you need to do anyway. Even when you are uncomfortable doing it.

Think of times in your life when you were uncomfortable with the conversation at hand.

How do you get comfortable being uncomfortable?
How do you power through?

_______________________________________________

_______________________________________________

_______________________________________________

_______________________________________________

_______________________________________________

_______________________________________________

_______________________________________________

Pillar Two
Do Not Hide in a
Crowd

Do not hide in the crowd when you're trying to elevate a conversation. It's vital to elevating tough and awkward conversations. This goes hand-in-hand with speaking your truth. It's risky to stand out from the crowd because it makes you vulnerable, but that doesn't make it any less important.

**Being self-aware will give you confidence and the strength you need to step away from the crowd.** It is safe and anonymous to hide in a crowd. It relieves us of the personal responsibility of elevating the conversation. But is it the right thing to do? Is that being your self-aware, authentic true self?

To elevate a tough conversation, again you must question your motivation and ask yourself if fear is the reason you are staying in the nameless, faceless crowd. **Do not let fear prevent you from stepping away from the crowd.**

Explain a time you let fear keep you in the crowd. Why?

________________________________________

________________________________________

________________________________________

________________________________________

________________________________________

All these memorable people claimed their place in history. By speaking their truths and stepping away from the crowd, they took great personal risks for their respective causes.

- Dr. Martin Luther King, Jr.

- Gandhi

- Harvey Milk

- Ruth Bader Ginsburg

- Harriet Tubman

- Jackie Robinson

- Nelson Mandela

- Rosa Parks

- Josephine Baker

- Melinda Gates

- Sally Ride

- Leonardo DiCaprio

- Fareed Zakaria

- Steve Jobs

- Stephen Colbert

- Temple Grandin

- Judy and Dennis Shepard

- Gary Zukav

Add those who have inspired you:

____________________________________________________

____________________________________________________

____________________________________________________

____________________________________________________

They elevated the conversation and refused to let fear silence their voices and cripple them into inaction.

And maybe you, too. Are you ready to step away from the crowd?

Stepping away from the crowd may be difficult at first. But you'll find once you do, others will join you.

Which brings me to our next pillar.

Pillar Three

Bring in Allies to
Have Your Back

Once you embrace the vulnerability and risk of speaking your truth and stepping out of the crowd, you'll find others will join you so you're not standing alone. There is strength in numbers.

You may be asking, "Aren't you just making a new crowd by encouraging others to join you?" That's certainly one way to look at it, but I choose to think of it like this: when you step away from the crowd and your voice is in the minority, you show authenticity and bravery in stepping out. This, my friends, is an admirable trait that people will want to emulate. You may find you may not be the only person with this point of view or this truth. Sometimes it only takes moving one stone to set the avalanche into motion.

When I was Ambassador, I encountered many oppressors and opponents who made attempts to thwart my progress on addressing corruption, improving human rights, accessing justice, and raising awareness of inequality in marginalized communities.

I wasn't alone in my endeavors for long, though. I didn't realize how many allies had my back, especially when I was under attack or addressing serious issues.

When I addressed a tough issue, those who wanted to keep the status quo would quickly attack me publicly. As those who benefitted from the status quo strengthened their public attacks, those who were negatively impacted began to rise up and stand alongside me. Among those standing with me were the diplomatic communities around the globe. An entire country was looking to me to say and do the right thing. And as a representative of the United States, I had a duty to speak and act.

A groundswell of support and respect grew.

By 2017, when I returned to the United States, I had developed a fluid relationship with both the public and private sectors in the country where I served and to this day still have people stop me on the streets or send me notes to say thank you for what you did for my country or what you did for my community. It gave me strength to keep speaking my truth.

This only works though if you have others' backs and build your bank of allies. Be there when others need you and speak out when they need you. Then when you speak your truth and your credibility is questioned, your allies will know it's time for them to rally and stand with you.

When was a time when you experienced others joining you in a cause you believed in? How did it affect your confidence going forward?

_______________________________________________

_______________________________________________

_______________________________________________

_______________________________________________

_______________________________________________

You see, in building your credibility by being a self-aware, authentic person who speaks their truth, you are really forming a network of allies who will have your back because they will support you when you are faced with attacks and challenges.

With an army of the right people behind you, you will be positioned to achieve the unachievable.

Pillar Four
Achieve the
Unachievable

When you achieve a win, it is amazing and empowering. No matter how big or small it is.

And it's not just your win. It's also a win for those on whose behalf you speak.

It's an amazing feeling to say the right thing, then act on it, and then know your efforts are helping others. From small community-building events and projects to spearheading worldwide efforts to alleviate suffering, achieving the unachievable is really at your fingertips. You will want to keep doing more and more once you experience success.

The thing that keeps you from achieving the unachievable is fear. Fear puts you back in that vulnerable place that makes it scary to try something new or something unimaginable.

The secret to achieving the unachievable is to take a risk. Set goals that are realistic and those you think are unachievable. You'll never know how much you can achieve unless you try. Think of how the Wright brothers felt when they built the first successful aircraft after countless failures. The world thought air flight couldn't be achieved. Thankfully, the Wright brothers thought otherwise!

I achieved the unachievable when I became
Ambassador to the Dominican Republic. Never
before in the Western Hemisphere had an openly
gay person been appointed Ambassador. I was a
small-town boy from East Texas and a married gay
man. I was not incredibly wealthy but I knew one
thing: after being with my husband for 23 years,
if Barack Obama was not re-elected President,
I would never be legally married to my husband
in my lifetime. It was a defining moment. We had
a tough conversation with ourselves about our
financial stability if we went "all in" with time and
money for the election and what it would mean for
us if we took a risk on the potential impact.

We asked ourselves how could we accomplish our goals when we weren't sure how to do it. We also knew that even if we were successful, we might obtain the right to be married, but what about an appointment in the administration? We worked incredibly hard to achieve this goal, I stepped out of my fear and comfort zone, but more importantly, I used all the pillars I've outlined in this book: I practiced self-awareness, spoke my truth, didn't hide in the crowd, and had many supporters at my back—including the President and Vice President of the United States—and allies around the globe I did not know I had.

52

As we Ambassadors headed out to our respective posts around the world, President Obama gave us one piece of advice: Listen.

*Just...listen.*

Listening skills you can apply immediately in your personal and professional life include the following:

- Be in the moment.

- Focus on the conversation.

- Summarize what the person says to you to show you're listening and understanding.

- Don't be distracted by phones, media, etc.

- Ask pertinent questions regarding the subject.

- Don't appear like you're waiting for your next turn to talk.

- Let your body language set the tone (demonstrate receptive body language).

- Ask yourself what do you think the intent of the person you are listening to is? Much of the time what we hear is not what is meant. Before you react ask yourself if what you heard is what they intentionally meant to say.

It's so simple, really. Good listeners listen beyond hearing words—tone, volume, body language, facial expressions, and intent. If you listen beyond words, it may change your strategy. It is only with this understanding that you can overcome roadblocks and proceed with what you set out to achieve.

This is tough and you may not always get it right.

Keep trying.

Keep listening.

Keep elevating tough conversations.

And now go and achieve the unachievable and have an amazing life full of adventures and experiences that results from being your true self!

# About the Author

Ambassador James (Wally) Brewster is the former U.S. Ambassador to the Dominican Republic serving under President Barack Obama. He made history as the first openly gay Ambassador to  serve the U.S. in the Western Hemisphere. He is an internationally recognized diplomat, C-suite executive, author, and motivational speaker. He advises top CEOs, political leaders, and governments on geopolitical strategy, global market dynamics, and market expansion. As a human rights activist, he challenges traditional thinking and fights to uplift the voices of the marginalized.

Follow Ambassador Brewster on social media:

 Wally Brewster

 @WallyBrewster

 ambbrewster

 The New Face of Diplomacy

 Ambassador James (Wally) Brewster